BLACK WIDOW SPIDER!

Willow Clark

WINDMILL BOOKS

New York

Published in 2011 by Windmill Books, LLC
303 Park Avenue South, Suite # 1280, New York, NY 10010-3657

Copyright © 2011 by Windmill Books, LLC

CREDITS:
Author: Willow Clark
Edited by: Jennifer Way
Designed by: Brian Garvey

Photo Credits: Cover George Grall/Getty Images; cover background © www. iStockphoto.com/Sabina Schaaf; pp. 4, 5, 6 (top, bottom), 7, 8, 9, 10-11, 13, 16, 22 (bottom) Shutterstock.com; pp. 12, 15, 20, 22 (top) © www.iStockphoto. com/Mark Kostich; p. 14 Michael Blann/Getty Images; p. 17 © www.iStockphoto. com/Andrew Clelland; p. 18 Ian Waldie/Getty Images; p. 19 © Robinson, James/ Animals Animals - Earth Scenes; p. 21 SIU/Getty Images.

Library of Congress Cataloging-in-Publication Data

Clark, Willow.
 Black widow spider! / by Willow Clark.
     p. cm. — (Animal danger zone)
 Includes index.
 ISBN 978-1-60754-959-8 (library binding) — ISBN 978-1-60754-968-0 (pbk.) — ISBN 978-1-60754-969-7 (6-pack)
 1. Black widow spider—Juvenile literature. I. Title.
 QL458.42.T54C53 2011
 595.4'4—dc22
                              2010004427

Manufactured in the United States of America

For more great fiction and nonfiction, go to windmillbooks.com.

CPSIA Compliance Information: Batch #S10W: For further information contact Windmill Books, New York, New York at 1-866-478-0556.

TABLE OF CONTENTS

Danger: Black Widow!

The female black widow spider is one of only a few North American spiders with a bite that is dangerous to people. The red markings on its **abdomen** are a warning to stay away or risk getting bitten.

Some black widow spiders live in the forests of North America.

4

The markings on a black widow's abdomen look like two bright red triangles that are touching each other.

The black widow spider is named for the fact that the female sometimes kills the male after they **mate**. A widow is a woman whose husband has died. Both male and female spiders of these **species** are called "black widow," however.

Insect

When people talk about creepy creatures, they often call everything a "bug." Many of these "bugs" are **insects**. But spiders are **arachnids**. One easy way to tell the difference is to look at the number of legs. Insects have six legs. Arachnids have eight legs.

There are about 40,000 species of spiders in the world. Of that number, the black widow spider is one of the three kinds of North American spiders that are harmful to people.

Arachnid

There are about 3,400 different kinds of spiders that live in North America. Most spiders are harmless to people.

There are three species of black widow. They are closely related and they live in some of the same places, so they are often talked about together.

Black widow spiders often live in tree stumps or near piles of branches or leaves.

Black widow spiders live all across the United States. Some even live in the desert.

The southern black widow is found as far south as Florida, as far north as New York, and as far west as Nevada. The northern black widow lives in the northeastern states from New York to southern Canada. The western black widow lives in the western states from Arizona to southwestern Canada.

Widow Spiders Around the World

The black widow has relatives that live all around the world. There are around 30 species of widow spiders in the world. Widow spiders live in South America, Europe, Africa, Asia, and the Middle East.

The red widow is bright reddish-orange and lives in Florida. The brown widow spider really gets around. It has been found in the United States, as well as Australia, South Africa, and Cyprus. No matter where they live, all widow spiders have venomous bites that can be harmful to people.

The Australian red-back spider looks a lot like its American cousin, which is shown here.

A spider's body is divided into two parts. The front part is called the **cephalothorax**. This is where the mouth, eyes, and legs are. The back part is the abdomen. This is where web-spinning parts called **spinnerets** are located.

An adult female black widow spider is about .5 inches (1.27 cm) long. An adult male is about .25 inches (.635 cm) long.

The red markings on this black widow spider show that it is a female.

Like many spiders, male and female black widows look different from one another. The female has a red hourglass-shaped marking on its abdomen. The male has yellow or red markings on its back and is lighter in color than the female.

Black widows are found in dark, undisturbed places. Outdoors they might be found around woodpiles, tree stumps, and low bushes. Sometimes they are found indoors in basements, garages, or crawl spaces.

Black widow spiders find dark places that are not bothered by people so they can build their strong webs.

Each of the black widow's eight legs is covered with tiny hairs that let it feel movements on its web

A spider's web plays many roles. It is the spider's home. It protects the spider from **predators**. It is a sticky trap for the spider's **prey**. Some spiders spin webs in a special pattern. Black widow spiders spin large, messy-looking webs.

Some of the insects that black widows eat are flies, mosquitoes, grasshoppers, beetles, and caterpillars.

Black widows prey on insects that become stuck in their webs. They bite the insect with their fangs. This injects venom into the insect. The venom turns the insect's insides into liquid. The spider then sucks up this liquid.

One animal that preys on the black widow is the mud-dauber wasp. This insect will catch and kill the black widow. It takes the spider back to its nest, where the wasp feeds the spider to its young.

Mud-dauber wasps are able to kill black widow spiders and bring them back to their nest to eat.

Black Widow Babies

During mating season, the male searches for a female. After mating, the female lays an egg sac in her web. The sac contains between 250 and 750 eggs. She guards the eggs until they hatch 14 to 30 days later.

Mating season is in the spring and summer. The female is shown here with her egg sac.

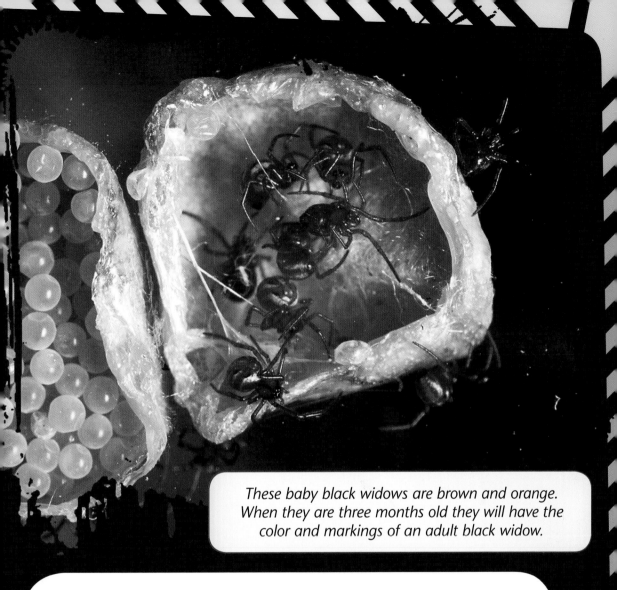

These baby black widows are brown and orange. When they are three months old they will have the color and markings of an adult black widow.

Baby spiders, or spiderlings, leave their mother's web after they hatch. Spiderlings are orange and brown. As they grow, they **molt**. Black widows are adults when they are about three months old.

Young children and people who have health problems are the most likely to get sick from a black widow's bite. Being careful is the best way to be safe from black widows. Look carefully before you pick up things in dark or rarely used rooms in a house or in woodsy areas outside.

Black widows live in dark, quiet places. Those are the places that people need to be the most careful.

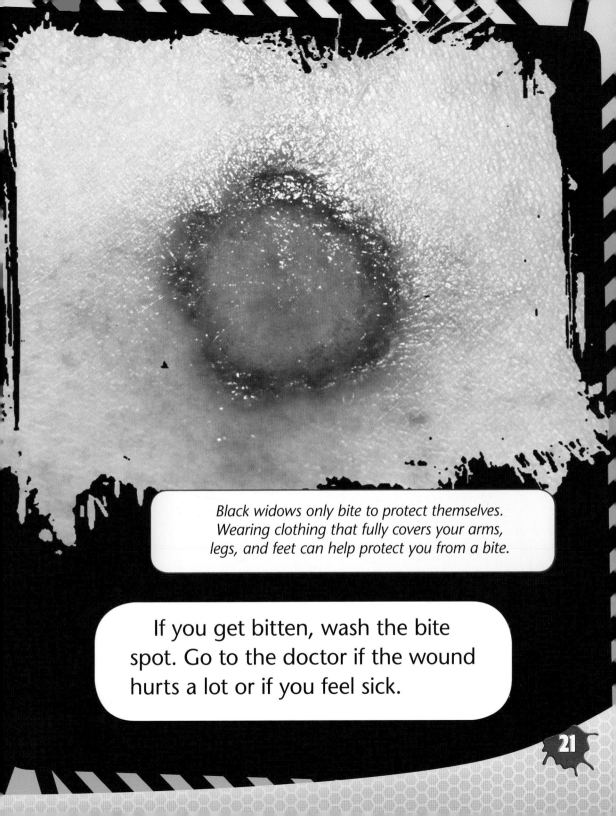

Black widows only bite to protect themselves. Wearing clothing that fully covers your arms, legs, and feet can help protect you from a bite.

If you get bitten, wash the bite spot. Go to the doctor if the wound hurts a lot or if you feel sick.

Did You Know?

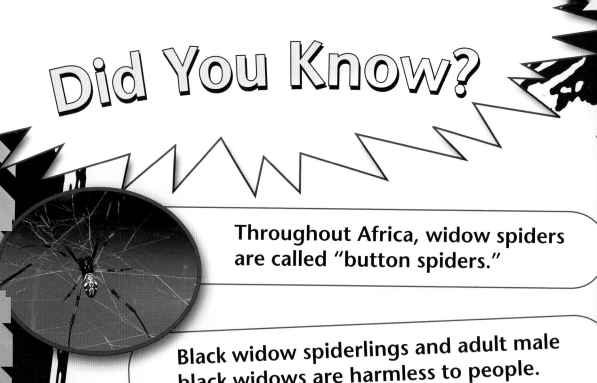

Throughout Africa, widow spiders are called "button spiders."

Black widow spiderlings and adult male black widows are harmless to people.

The messy style of web that the black widow makes is also called a cobweb.

The female black widow's venom is 15 times stronger than that of a rattlesnake!

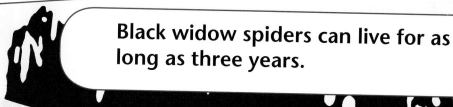

Black widow spiders can live for as long as three years.

GLOSSARY

abdomen (AB-duh-mun) The large, rear part of an spider's body.

arachnid (uh-RAK-nid) A type of animal, such as a spider, scorpion, or tick.

cephalothorax (seh-fuh-low-THOR-aks) An area on the front part the spider's body.

insect (IN-sekt) Small animals that often have six legs and wings.

mate (MAYT) To come together to make babies.

molt (MOHLT) To shed hair, feathers, shell, horns, or skin.

predators (PREH-duh-terz) Animals that kill other animals for food.

prey (PRAY) An animal that is hunted by another animal for food.

species (SPEE-sheez) One kind of living thing. All people are one species.

spinnerets (spih-nuh-RETS) Parts, located on the rear of the spider's body, that make silk for their webs.

venomous (VEH-nuh-mis) Having a poisonous bite.

INDEX

READ MORE

Cooper, Jason. *Black Widow Spiders.* Vero Beach, FL: Rourke Publishing, 2006.

Lunis, Natalie. *Deadly Black Widows.* New York: Bearport Publishing, 2008.

Miller, Heather. *Bugs—Black Widow.* Farmington Hills, MI: KidHaven Press, 2004.

WEB SITES

For Web resources related to the subject of this book, go to: www.windmillbooks.com/weblinks and select this book's title.